60
SUPER
SIMPLE
TRAVEL GAMES

By Jill Smolinski

Illustrated by Leo Abbett

LOWELL HOUSE JUVENILE

LOS ANGELES

CONTEMPORARY BOOKS

CHICAGO

Copyright © 1997 by RGA Publishing Group, Inc.
All rights reserved. No part of this work may be reproduced or transmitted in any form or by any means, electronic or mechanical, including photocopying and recording, or by any information storage or retrieval system, except as may be expressly permitted by the 1976 Copyright Act or in writing by the publisher.

Publisher: Jack Artenstein
Vice President, Juvenile Division: Elizabeth Amos
Director of Publishing Services: Rena Copperman
Managing Editor, Juvenile Division: Lindsey Hay
Editor in Chief: Amy Downing
Art Director: Lisa Theresa Lenthall
Cover photograph: Ann Bogart

Lowell House books can be purchased at special discounts when ordered in bulk for premiums and special sales. Contact Department TC at the following address:
Lowell House Juvenile
2020 Avenue of the Stars, Suite 300
Los Angeles, CA 90067

Library of Congress Catalog Card Number is available.

ISBN: 1-56565-584-2

Manufactured in the United States of America

10 9 8 7 6 5 4 3 2

CONTENTS

FAMILY
CAR RITUALS

Nothing brings a family closer together than doing the same strange stuff . . . over and over again! You can make up car rituals that are all your own. A ritual may last for just the length of one car trip, but some could wind up becoming a permanent part of your family's history.

WHAT YOU'LL NEED
• a family

HOW TO PLAY

❶ When it comes to car rituals, the crazier the better! Some people hold their breath when passing through a tunnel. Others lift their feet over railroad tracks. Here you'll find some ideas for starting your own family rituals while traveling.

- Pick a taboo term. If someone accidentally says it, he or she will have to take the consequences (a tickle, having to sing a song, or just everyone cheering). Taboo terms are always more fun when they tie in with your trip. For instance, if you're going to visit your grandparents, make *grandma* the taboo word. Other good taboo terms/phrases: *bathroom, bored, car, hot, sleeping, book,* and *"when will we get there?"*

- Watch for milestones. A milestone is a big moment on a trip, and your family can celebrate when it happens by cheering, singing a song, or getting a snack. How about making it a milestone when your car's odometer—the instrument that shows how many miles you've driven—reaches a hundred mile mark, which means the last two digits are 00. Other milestones can be coming to a town, seeing a limousine or other rare car, crossing over a bridge, or spotting a helicopter.

• Get inspired by something that happens on your trip. What if you think you'll never make it to the next rest stop, so your family claps like crazy when you do? You might wind up always clapping at rest stops. Suppose you pass a stinky skunk just as an airplane flies overhead? Maybe the members of your family will forever hold their noses when they see an airplane—whether or not a skunk is around!

❷ Keep a record of your favorite car rituals. Even if the memories of your vacation fade, your rituals will live on and on.

2

WARMLY,
COLDLY

A car ride that's going slowly will soon have you acting crabbily! Luckily, here's a game that'll have you playing happily . . . quickly!

WHAT YOU'LL NEED

• three or more players • several sheets of paper
• pens or pencils (one per player) • paper bag

HOW TO PLAY

❶ Each player tears a piece of paper into four squares.

❷ On each square, players write an adverb, a word that describes how something is done. Adverbs usually end in *ly*, such as *secretly, quickly, angrily, curiously, busily,* and so on. Squares are folded, then mixed up in a paper bag.

❸ One player goes first as the actor. He or she selects an adverb from the bag, keeping it a secret from the others. It's okay if the actor selects his or her own word.

❹ Now the actor tries to perform the word, never speaking or writing words. Sounds—such as grunting or giggling—are allowed. The actor can also use props. For example, if the adverb was intelligently, the actor might put on a pair of glasses and read a book.

❺ The players call out guesses. The actor nods if players are getting "warm"—that is, getting closer to guessing the adverb—or gives a shake of the head if the guessers are getting "cold."

❻ The first player to guess the adverb scores a point.

❼ The game continues so that each player gets a chance to be the actor four times. The player with the most points when the bag of adverbs is empty is the winner.

BOX

FLIPPING

Stuck sitting at a table with nothing to do? Here's a simple activity that you're sure to flip for—whether you're at a restaurant or even waiting for your airplane food to arrive!

WHAT YOU'LL NEED
• two or more players • small matchbox

HOW TO PLAY

❶ Set the matchbox at the edge of the table. About a third of it should be sticking over the edge.

❷ Get in the ready position—your index finger and thumb touch, as though you're saying "okay." The tip of your thumb should be right beneath the edge of the box.

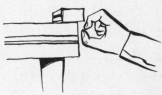

❸ Now release your finger and flick the matchbox upward. Take a look at how it landed.

If it landed . . .	You get . . .
top side down	0 points
top side up	1 point
on its side	3 points
on one end	5 points

❹ Take turns matching your box-flipping skills against another player. Who got the most points by the time the meal arrived?

NOBODY
NOSE!

Who can find all four cards first? Don't be the last player who nose, or you'll be out of the game!

WHAT YOU'LL NEED

• **three to six players** • **six postcards** • **scissors**

BEFORE YOU LEAVE

❶ Make special Nobody Nose game cards that will remind you of your trip every time you use them. To do this, you'll need six postcards. Choose ones that have colorful scenes on one side but are nearly blank on the other. Many hotels give away free postcards—just ask!

❷ Cut each postcard into four equal pieces so that you have a deck of 24 cards.

> **NOTE:** *Never use scissors in a moving vehicle, especially a car, bus, or train. Cut out what you need before you leave.*

HOW TO PLAY

❶ Players take turns being the dealer. The dealer gives an equal number of cards to each player, photo side down. Make sure that you don't show your cards to anyone else!

❷ Take a close look at your cards. Do you have four that match? If not, choose one card that you don't want and hand it facedown to the player on your left. All other players should do the same.

❸ Add the new card to your hand, then select another card to discard. The object is to find four cards that, if pieced together, would complete one of the cut-up postcards.

❹ When this happens—*shhhhh!* Don't say a thing. Instead, just quietly place your finger alongside your nose.

❺ It's up to the other players to race to do the same. The last person to notice and touch his or her nose is out of the game.

5

FEELIES
ON WHEELIES

Have you ever tried to remember something, but you just can't put your finger on it? That's what this game is all about!

WHAT YOU'LL NEED

• two or more players • 15 small items per player • paper bags (one per player)
• several sheets of paper • pens or pencils (one per player)
• timer or watch with a second hand • shoebox lid

HOW TO PLAY

❶ First, everyone collects 15 different small items and stores them in a paper bag. You can do this as you travel on the road. Make sure to keep your items secret from everyone else! Some possible items: small rocks, toys, coins, or school supplies (but nothing sharp or that can be squished out of shape).

❷ Hand out paper and a pen or pencil to everyone. Number each person's bag 1, 2, 3, and so on.

❸ Pass your bag to the player next to you.

❹ Set a timer. All players now have one minute to use their fingers to try to feel as many items as they can in the bag they're holding. No peeking!

❺ Now it's time to put your memory to the test. On your piece of paper, record the number on the bag you're holding. Then write down as many items in the bag that you're able to recognize and remember. Each player does the same.

❻ After about three minutes, all players pass their bags again. The game repeats until every player has had a chance to try to identify the items in each bag (except his or her own).

❼ The player with the bag labeled number 1 spreads his or her items out on a flat surface such as a shoebox lid. The player compares his or her list against the contents, getting one point for each correct object that's written down. Subtract a point for any item listed that wasn't actually in the bag.

❽ Repeat this step with all the bags. Tally up the number of correct answers that each player got for each bag and compare the scores. Who got the most total points? Who scored the most for each bag? Based on scores, which bag had objects that were the hardest to identify by feel?

SCRAMBLED

SAYINGS

Can't guess the name of this mystery message when the letters are all mixed up?

WHAT YOU'LL NEED

• two players or teams • several sheets of paper
• pen or pencil • tray or box lid • timer

GETTING READY

❶ Start with three pieces of paper. With a ruler, divide each of them into 36 squares (6 lines up and down, 4 lines across).

❷ Now write the alphabet on each piece of paper, one letter per square (you'll have 10 blank spaces left over). Cut along the lines.

NOTE: *Never use scissors in a moving vehicle, especially a car, bus, or train. Cut out what you need before you leave.*

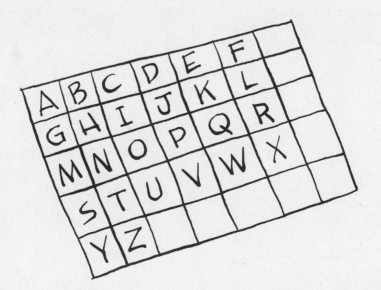

HOW TO PLAY

❶ Start by secretly picking out a song, movie, TV show, or famous saying that you think will be familiar to the other player or team.

❷ Choose some of the key words in the mystery phrase to scramble. For instance, if you choose the tune "Take Me Out to the Ball Game," you might want to mix up the letters to *take, out,* and *ball game.* If it's something shorter—like "Happy Birthday"—you might just want to scramble *birthday* and leave *happy* as a clue.

❸ Sift through the game pieces to find the letters that make up the words you've selected. It may be necessary to write extra letters on the blank leftover squares.

❹ Now write out the other words—in this sample, *me, to,* and *the*—on blank squares, one word per square.

❺ Put all the letters and words face up on a tray or a box lid. Hand it to the other player or team and give one hint, such as "It's a TV show," or "It's a song that is sung to you once a year."

❻ Set the timer, and the other player or team has five minutes to move the pieces around to puzzle it out.

❼ If you want to keep score, use the system below.

If the puzzle is solved in . . .	The team receives . . .
less than 1 minute	10 points
1 to 2 minutes	5 points
2 to 3 minutes	3 points
3 to 4 minutes	2 points
4 to 5 minutes	1 point

AUNT SALLY

IS STRANGE

So you think that your relatives are weird? Wait until you play this crazy game about an Aunt Sally whose love of words is so very strange.

WHAT YOU'LL NEED
• **two or more players**

HOW TO PLAY

❶ Start by selecting a secret word formula. It can be anything you decide, such as words that have a certain letter, that have two syllables, that contain double letters, that have three vowels, that don't have an *e*, and so on.

❷ The game goes into play when you first say, "My Aunt Sally is strange . . ." then give the reasons why. The reasons are actually clues to the formula you chose.

❸ So after you say, "My Aunt Sally is strange . . ." —if your formula is words that contain the letter *f*, for instance—you might add, "She loves fudge but hates other sweets."

❹ Players then follow up with questions about what your aunt likes so they can figure out the secret. A player might ask, "Does she like sports?" Of course you'd say no, since the word *sports* doesn't contain an *f*. Then be sure to give an extra hint, such as adding that she likes football. If someone asks, "Does she like butterflies?" you'd say, "Yes, and she also likes daffodils," or "but she doesn't like ants."

❺ Players take turns asking questions that you respond to based on your formula. Your Aunt Sally might like beef but not cows, sofas but not couches, fish but not sharks . . . you get the idea!

❻ The first player to correctly call out the formula wins the game and is the next to have a strange Aunt Sally.

S Q U I G G L E

A R T

It's a squiggle, it's a scrawl—no, it's a great work of art! Here's your chance to set the art world on fire by making something out of nothing.

WHAT YOU'LL NEED

• two or more players • markers or colored pencils (several per player)
• several sheets of paper • timer

HOW TO PLAY

❶ All players start with a piece of paper on their laps and their eyes closed. Now, everyone draws a squiggle on his or her paper—no peeking!

❷ Now trade papers and look at the drawing in front of you.

❸ Set a timer for three minutes. Get a pen that's a different color than the squiggle, and add to the drawing to make it look like a real object. The goal is to use as few extra lines as possible. In fact, you may think the drawing already looks like something, so you might not want to do anything.

❹ Write what the object is on the back of the paper. Now trade your works of art back. Vote to see who created the best drawing using the least extra lines.

THE GREAT

PLATE COUNT

9

What's a car trip without a license plate game? Start counting numbers on license plates instead of just counting the hours until you get to your destination.

WHAT YOU'LL NEED

• two or more players • several sheets of paper
• pens or pencils (one per player)

HOW TO PLAY

❶ Get ready to do some fast adding! Start by pointing to the first car that passes by. Call out the numbers that appear on its license plate. For instance, suppose the license plate is SMO135. You'd say, "One, three, five."

❷ Quickly add the numbers in your head. One plus three plus five equals nine. Your score now stands at nine. Write it on your piece of paper.

❸ It's the other player's turn to claim the next car and add up its single digits. Make sure you're using a car only once, and that no two players claim the same plate.

❹ Keep taking turns and add each license plate's numbers to your existing score.

❺ The first player to find enough numbers that add up to 100 wins the game. You must reach 100 exactly—no going over! If your score is 95 or higher, however, instead of adding up all the digits on a license plate, you may be able to pick just a single number to reach your goal.

SIGN
SEARCH

So what if you can't do board games on the road? Instead, try your hand at a billboard game that has you finding letters on signs from A to Z—and everything in between.

WHAT YOU'LL NEED

• two or more players • several sheets of paper
• pens or pencils (one per player)

HOW TO PLAY

❶ Hand out paper and a pen or a pencil to each player.

❷ As you drive, be on the lookout for signs. They can be billboards, road signs, store fronts, bus stop posters—anything in writing that doesn't move. (That means the signs on buses, car license plates, or bumper stickers don't count.) The goal of the game is to find all the letters of the alphabet in proper order on the signs you pass by.

❸ The letter you're looking for can appear anywhere in the word. Start your search with *A*. When you see it, point to the sign and call out the word that it's in. This claims it as your own. Players can choose a letter from the same sign, but not the same word.

❹ Then write the word on your paper, circling the letter like this:

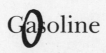

Ga**s**oline

❺ Now look for *B*. When playing Sign Search, you can use more than one letter in a word, as long as the letters appear in proper order. As an example, if you're searching for *B* and you see a sign that says BACK SOON, you can circle both the *B* and the next letter on your list, *C*.

❻ The first player to find letters from *A* to *Z* is the winner.

MAGAZINE
SCAVENGER HUNT

You don't have to run all over town for a scavenger hunt. Just grab a magazine and a pen—and be the first to cross off all the items on your list.

WHAT YOU'LL NEED
• two or more players • several sheets of paper • pens or pencils (one per player)
• timer • a magazine for each player, preferably similar, such as all fashion, news, entertainment, and so on

HOW TO PLAY

❶ First, make a list of about 20 items that you'll try to find in your scavenger hunt. To do this, players take turns suggesting things that might be found in the pages of a magazine. Some ideas to get you started: ice cream in a cup, a red car, mascara, a TV celebrity, a baby, a bicycle, a swimsuit, glasses, a ring, flowers, soup, and a hat.

❷ Make sure every player has a copy of the list.

❸ Set a timer for 5 or 10 minutes.

❹ At the word go, flip through your magazine trying to find as many of the items on the list as you can. When you spot something you need, circle it on your list and write down the page number it appears on.

❺ The first player to find all the items first, or the player with the most items at the end of the time limit, is the winner.

❻ Now make a new list, grab some more magazines, and play again!

R A D I O
B I N G O

It's okay if your parents like country music, while you prefer rock. Everyone will love listening to the radio as you fill in special Bingo cards. You'll never fight over a radio station again!

WHAT YOU'LL NEED
**• two or more players • several sheets of paper
• pens or pencils (one per player) • ruler • radio**

HOW TO PLAY

❶ With a ruler, each player divides a piece of paper into 16 squares (3 lines up and down, 3 lines across). This is your Radio Bingo card.

❷ On each space, write something that you would expect to hear on the radio. For example, you might make one card with only singers, and another with titles of songs, products, names of people in the news, sound effects, and so on.

❸ Now one player gathers all the cards and mixes them facedown. Each player picks a card—you might get your own or a card someone else made.

❹ Ready to rock and roll? Just turn on the radio.

❺ When one of the items on your Radio Bingo card comes up on the radio, announce it to the other players. Then cross it off your card by drawing a big X through the middle. Or if you want to use the card again, use a small mark like your initials or a symbol.

❻ The first player to cross out every space in a row either across, up and down, or diagonally wins.

A MY NAME
IS ALEX

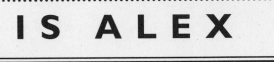

Get ready for a case of the giggles as you fill in the blanks on a super-silly sentence that's called A My Name Is Alex. G this game is goofy!

WHAT YOU'LL NEED
• **two or more players**

HOW TO PLAY

❶ Start by saying, "*A* my name is . . ."

❷ Then recite the line that you see here. Replace the underlined words with ones that begin with the letter *A*. How crazy can you be? Let's see!

> *A* my name is <u>a name</u>. My wife's (husband's) name is <u>a name</u>. We live in <u>a place</u>. We like <u>adjective noun</u>. Isn't that a <u>description of the situation</u>?

Here's a sample: "*A* my name is Alex. My wife's name is Abby. We live in Albuquerque. We like angry alligators. Isn't that awful?"

❸ The next player gets *B*. She might say, "*B* my name is Bernice. My husband's name is Barney. We live in a bell tower. We like big bees. Isn't that bizarre?"

❹ Take turns until you've made it all the way through the alphabet. (When you get to *X*, you might want to make a rule that you can do *ex* as well, or skip the letter altogether.)

❺ Now go ahead and start again, this time with another player taking *A*. Remember to be as silly as possible!

HUG-A-BUG

Who wants to hug a bug? In this game, players hurry to come up with the right words before they become a bug.

WHAT YOU'LL NEED
• two or more players

HOW TO PLAY

1 One person begins by being the Bug.

2 The Bug calls out a three-letter word. It can be anything, such as hug, all, hop, tot, or man, just as long as it has three letters.

3 At the same time, the Bug taps the first player on his or her left, then starts to count to 10.

4 The player must quickly say three words that begin with the letters from the Bug's word. For instance, if the Bug says, "top," then the player could say, "toy, open, potato." Sounds too easy? Another way to play is to require that all the words are somehow connected. "Top" could be "tomatoes, onions, potatoes," because these are all foods. How about "touch, open, pull"? All verbs!

5 If the player hasn't said all three words by the time the Bug counts to 10, the Bug shouts, "Hug-a-Bug!" Then the player gets a point and takes over as the Bug.

6 A player who gets three points is out of the game. The last remaining player is the King or Queen of the Bugs!

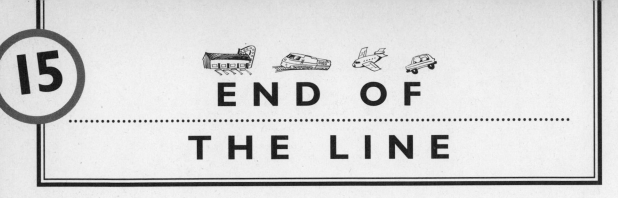

END OF
THE LINE

When the competing player gets to the end of his or her turn, it's just the beginning for you! End of the Line is a great game for killing time when you think you'll never get to the end of your trip.

WHAT YOU'LL NEED
• **two or more players**

HOW TO PLAY

❶ Choose a general category, such as rock stars, celebrities, cities, movies, things you find outside, sports, characters in books, or foods.

❷ Once the category is chosen, the first player names something in that category. If your category is "fictional characters," for instance, you might start with "Peter Piper."

❸ The next player follows with a name in which any of the words in it begin with the last letter of the word just said. Sound tricky? Go back to the Peter Piper example. The next word would start with *r*, for Piper. How about Rin Tin Tin? Or Speed Racer?

❹ Play continues until someone can't think of a word. At that point, it's anyone's guess. The first player to shout out a correct answer wins the round.

❺ Now you can switch to a new category and start all over again.

Helpful Hint: Once you get started, you may find that many names and places end in the letters *e* or *s*. After a certain point in the game, you might want to outlaw any name that ends with one of these letters, or agree to use the next to last letter when *e* or *s* titles run out.

K I S S E S
A N D   H U G S

Some people like to sign their letters with a hug and a kiss, using an X and an O. Can you manage to get lots of kisses without the hugs?

WHAT YOU'LL NEED
• two players • several sheets of paper • different colored pen for each player • scarf or other item to use as a blindfold

HOW TO PLAY

❶ Draw 25 Xs (hugs) and 50 Os (kisses) on a piece of paper in a random pattern. The kisses and hugs should be about the same size.

❷ Put your paper of kisses and hugs on a table or on a steady surface on your lap. Tie a scarf or a T-shirt around your eyes as a blindfold. Get a pen ready!

❸ Now draw one continuous line through the page. The line can curve and can be as long or as short as you want. As soon as you lift your pen from the paper, your turn is over. The object is to pass your pen through as many kisses as possible, without getting any hugs.

❹ Remove your blindfold and count how many kisses and hugs your line passed through. "Passing through" includes touching *any* part of the X or O. You score one point for every kiss (O) but must subtract one for every hug (X). You may find that when you draw a very long line, you possibly earn more points—but you stand to lose more as well.

❺ Now the other player takes a turn using the same paper but a different colored pen. Use a new paper with Xs and Os after both players have had a turn. After three rounds, the player with the most points is the winner and deserves a great big hug!

ROAD TRIP

Roll the die and move your car along a racetrack that you construct. The first player to go the distance is the winner!

WHAT YOU'LL NEED

• two to four players • one die • highlighter marker • pen • box lid
• a tiny game piece for each player, such as a bead, a rock, or a coin

HOW TO PLAY

❶ First make the game board for your "road trip" using the inside of a large box lid. Start with your highlighter pen in the upper left corner of the lid. Draw and color in a thick line that continues like a long, winding road. Your road will finish at the lower right corner.

❷ Now mark off every inch or so on your road until you have exactly 100 squares. (Your squares will probably vary in size.)

❸ Number each square 1 through 100.

❹ Now randomly pick squares in which to write these instructions:

- rest stop: lose a turn
- carpool lane: get double points next turn
- flat tire: go back five squares
- car sick: back to start!

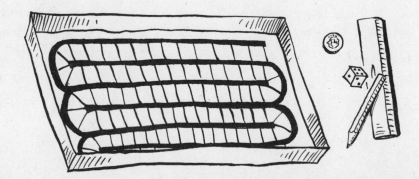

You can also make up your own penalties or bonus spots. The more you include, the more action-packed your game will be. (Don't fill every square, though, or you'll never finish playing!)

❺ To play, the first player throws the die and moves his or her "car" the number of squares, or "miles," shown on the die. Follow any special instructions on the square. Then it's the next player's turn.

❻ If a player lands on a square already occupied by someone else, the player must immediately roll again. He or she then goes back the number of spaces on the die.

❼ The first car to reach the last space—100 miles—is the winner. This space must be reached with an exact roll of the die.

OH, NO!

KO NO!

Chinese children often play Ko No using pebbles and a game board scratched into the sand. Here's a version of this ancient game that you can take with you on your travels.

WHAT YOU'LL NEED

• two players • four game pieces (two each of something that is the same) such as rocks, coins, or buttons • paper • pen or pencil • ruler

HOW TO PLAY

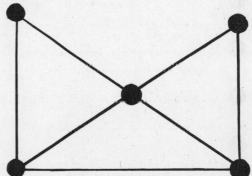

❶ Use your ruler to draw a 6-inch vertical line on the right- and left-hand sides of your paper, 6 inches apart. Connect them with a line at the bottom.

❷ Now draw two diagonal lines connecting the corners so that your game board looks like what you see here.

❸ Flip a coin to see which player goes first. If you're first, you place your game pieces at each of the two top corners. The other player takes the bottom corners.

❹ Now move one of your pieces to the center spot. The other player counters by moving a piece to the empty space created when you made your first move. This is when the strategy of Ko No really begins. The object of the game is to try to corner your opponent so that he or she is unable to make a move.

❺ The game continues with players taking turns moving their pieces to the one space that's left empty. This isn't checkers, though: no jumping allowed. All moves must be along a marked line from one space to another right next to it. The first player to block the other is the winner.

QUICK
PICKUP

Comb the beach for tiny shells or a park for pebbles. Then try this game, which puts your quick reflexes to the test.

WHAT YOU'LL NEED
• two or more players • 20 small shells, pebbles, or
dried beans, plus 10 for each player • a bowl

HOW TO PLAY

❶ Everyone sits in a circle around a bowl filled with 20 shells or other playing pieces.

❷ Make sure each player has 10 playing pieces, not including those in the bowl.

❸ Sit cross-legged with your pile of shells in front of you.

❹ Place a shell on the back of your hand. With a quick motion, toss the shell into the air by jerking your hand up. With the same hand, grab another shell from the pile on your lap. Now catch the falling piece. It sounds like a lot to do all at once, but with a little practice you'll be a pro in no time.

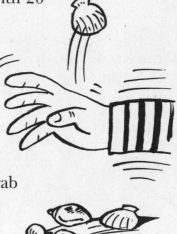

❺ If you succeed in getting both shells, you can also take one from the bowl. If you miss either shell, however, you must donate one of the shells from your supply to the bowl.

❻ Players can take turns, going around in a circle, or all just play at the same time. The game continues until the bowl is emptied of shells. If you have to quit before that happens, the player with the most shells is considered the winner.

MAGIC
CUP

Just one cup contains the stone. Can you guess which one? This is a great game to play surfside when you're tired of making sandcastles.

WHAT YOU'LL NEED
• two or more players • four clear plastic cups • sand
• a small stone (or other tiny object such as a shell, bead, or marble)

HOW TO PLAY

❶ Place a stone in the bottom of a clear plastic cup. Fill the cup to the top with sand. Pour sand into three other cups, but don't put anything else inside. Now set them out and say, "Show me the magic cup!"

❷ The other player must point to the cup that contains the stone. Once he or she indicates a choice, empty out the cup. If the stone is not there, keep trying until the magic cup is found.

❸ The person guessing earns points based on how many tries it took to find the magic cup. Scoring is as follows:

first try	10 points
second try	6 points
third try	4 points
fourth try	0 points

❹ Take turns hiding and finding the stone. The first player to score 50 points wins.

SUPER SIMPLE
SOLITAIRE

Solitaire is a great game to play when you're alone, but it usually requires table space. This version is so compact, you can play it anywhere—in a car, an airplane, or even in a one-person kayak!

WHAT YOU'LL NEED
• one player • deck of playing cards • paper • pen or pencil

HOW TO PLAY

❶ Shuffle the deck and hold the cards in your hands facedown.

❷ Now turn the cards over one at a time, setting them in a pile next to you or in your lap. As you do this, count aloud, "ace, two, three, four," and so on. Repeat this as you go through the deck, saying one word for every card. When you get to "king," just start over again with "ace."

❸ The object of the game is to get through the entire deck without ever saying the same name of the card that you're turning over. When that happens— suppose you're saying "queen" while you're turning over a queen—that round is over. Your score is the number of cards that you've already turned up.

❹ Play five rounds, then tally up your score. A perfect score is 260 (52 cards in the deck times 5 games). Try to beat your best game or another player's highest score.

MANCALA
MANIA

People have been playing this strategy game for thousands of years. Although kids used to hack their game boards from logs, you can make a simplified version from an ordinary egg carton.

WHAT YOU'LL NEED

• two players • egg carton • two small paper cups • tape • 48 small stones

HOW TO PLAY

1 Carefully tear off and discard the top of an egg carton. Set a paper cup on each end of the carton so that the cup sits flat.

2 Each player claims one side of the egg carton and the paper cup to his or her left, which is called the Kahala.

3 Each player puts four stones in his or her six holes, but not in the Kahala.

4 Flip a coin or play a quick game of Odds and Evens (page 35) to decide who goes first.

5 Start by picking up all the stones in any hole on your side. By moving around the board to your right, put the stones one by one in each hole. If you reach the end of your side but are still holding stones, place one stone in your Kahala.

6 Still holding one or more stones? You can continue counterclockwise, putting stones in your opponent's holes. Never, however, place stones in his or her Kahala. If the last stone that you move lands in your own Kahala, you get another turn.

7 If the last stone lands in an empty hole on your own side of the board, you get to take all the stones out of the hole right across from it. Put these stones in your Kahala, along with the stone used to capture them. If the hole across from your empty hole is also empty, put your stone in your Kahala.

8 No touching stones in the hole to count them! Once you touch a hole, you have to use it. The game is over when all six holes on a player's side are empty.

9 The remaining player then empties all the stones from his or her side. These are placed in that player's Kahala. The winner is the person with the most stones in his or her Kahala.

TINY

WHITE LIE

Each player takes turns telling a true story that includes one tiny white lie. Can the other players guess which part isn't the truth?

WHAT YOU'LL NEED

• two or more players • several sheets of paper
• pens or pencils (one per player) • timer

HOW TO PLAY

❶ Face the other players and set the timer for 30 seconds. Then tell a true tale—that is, almost true. While you're telling your story about, say, what you had for breakfast, tuck in one tiny white lie. You might say that you put butter on your toast when you actually ate it plain, for example, or that your mom snuck some of your cereal when she really didn't.

❷ The other players will be watching you closely to see if they can tell when you lie. After your story is over, the other players will try to uncover your little untruth. Each writes a guess on a sheet of paper.

❸ After the players turn in their guesses, read them all aloud; then reveal your little white lie. Did anyone get it right? If so, he or she gets a point. If you fooled everyone, then you earn a point.

❹ Now it's someone else's turn to tell a tricky tale. The player with the most points after everyone has had a chance to tell his or her story is the winner.

ODDS AND
EVENS

Need to decide who goes first or who gets the front seat? This game lets you choose up sides fairly by letting your fingers do the talking.

WHAT YOU'LL NEED
• **two players**

HOW TO PLAY

❶ One player takes "evens" and the other "odds." At the same time, both players make a fist and say, "One, two, three . . ." Then each player shows any number of fingers (no thumbs) on one hand.

❷ Count up the total fingers between you and your opponent. One, three, five, or seven means the person who claimed "odds" is the winner. Two, four, six, or eight gives the victory to whoever claimed "evens."

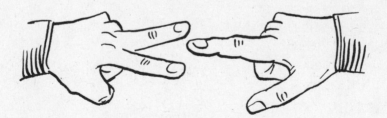

THE LAST
STRAW

This game takes more skill than luck. It's a favorite strategy game played throughout the world.

WHAT YOU'LL NEED
• **two players** • **21 straws** • **box lid**

HOW TO PLAY

❶ Lay 21 straws side by side so that they form a long row, like you see here. If you're in a car, train, or on a plane, lay the straws in a box lid to keep them from rolling away.

❷ Players take turns picking up onc, two, or three straws at a time. The object is to leave just one straw on the last turn.

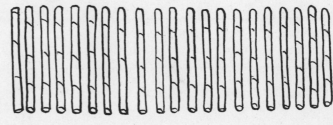

❸ The player who is left with the final straw loses the game.

JUST
LIKE OURS

Take a good look at the people in cars next to yours on the road. You'll be surprised to find that in many ways their cars are just like yours!

WHAT YOU'LL NEED

**• two or more players • timer or watch with second hand
• several sheets of paper • pen or pencil (one per player)**

HOW TO PLAY

❶ Set a timer for 60 seconds. Now point to a car and say, "That car is just like ours!"

❷ As fast as you can, call out all the many ways your two cars are similar. Keep count as you go. Here's a sample of what you might say: "One, they're both red. Two, they have a *J* in their license plates. Three, there are four people inside, too. Four, both our dads have red hair . . ." Keep going until the timer goes off.

❸ The other players should watch closely in case you accidentally call off something that's not really the same. If that happens, they must point it out right away so that you can subtract it from your count.

❹ Now it's time for the next player to compare the car with another. Players should keep track of their score, which is the total of how many similarities they found for each car. At the end of three rounds, the player with the highest score is the winner.

S L A P
S T I C K S

What's a vacation without an occasional Popsicle® or ice-cream treat? After you're done, play this simple stick-breaking game.

WHAT YOU'LL NEED
• **two players**
• **Popsicle stick for each player per round**

HOW TO PLAY

❶ One player holds his or her stick by placing one hand on either end.

❷ Now grasp your stick at the tip. Try to break your friend's stick by striking it as hard as you can with your own stick.

❸ Take turns hitting each other's sticks until someone wins by breaking an opponent's stick.

BEETLE

BUG

Here's your chance to start a bug collection, one beetle body part at a time!

WHAT YOU'LL NEED

• **two to six players** • **one die** • **shoebox** • **several sheets of paper**
• **pens or pencils (one per player)**

HOW TO PLAY

❶ The youngest player gets to roll first and tries to throw a 1, tossing the die into the shoebox. Each player gets one roll per turn.

❷ When a player throws a 1, he or she gets to begin drawing a beetle. Numbers must be thrown in sequence, so if you toss a 2, you can't do anything until you get a 1 first. Each time you toss the right number on the die, you get to draw part of your beetle.

When you throw a . . .	You get to draw . . .
1	the beetle's body
2	the head
3	three legs on one side
3	three legs on the other side
4	two feelers
5	two eyes
6	the beetle's big smile!

❸ The first player to draw the smile and complete the beetle is the winner.

PICTURE
THIS!

Think you're pretty good at drawing? It's often simple to draw objects like cats or houses. But how do you put an idea in pictures? This game puts your drawing talents to the challenge!

WHAT YOU'LL NEED
• **three or more players** • **several sheets of paper**
• **pens or pencils (one per player)**
• **crayons or markers (optional)**

HOW TO PLAY

❶ One player chooses a category. Here are some to get you started, or you can make up your own.

- famous scenes in history
- great places
- really scary things
- songs
- movies
- famous people

❷ Players begin by each folding a sheet of paper in half, then opening it back up again.

BLOWIN' _IN THE WIND_ – J.B._

❸ Use the top half of your paper only. Draw a picture based on the category. Suppose you chose a song, for instance. You might try to draw the song "Colors of the Wind" by drawing swirly lines to look like wind, then coloring them in—or any way you think you can illustrate the song title.

❹ Players pass their drawings to the person on their left. This player tries to figure out the actual song that the picture is supposed to represent, writing a guess and his or her initials at the very bottom of the page. The player then folds the paper up about an inch so that no one can see the written answer.

❺ Each picture is then passed to the next player until everyone has had a chance to see every picture and make a guess.

❻ Drawings are returned to the artist. One by one, the artist opens them and reads the guesses aloud. Who got the most right? Which pictures were the easiest or the hardest to figure out?

RING
TOSS

"Here we go loop-de-loo, here we go loop-de-lie. Here we go loop-de-loo . . . all as we go on a drive!"

WHAT YOU'LL NEED

• **curtain ring or similar-weight ring** • **stick about 8 inches long**
• **string about 20 inches long** • **tape**

HOW TO PLAY

❶ Tie one end of the string around the ring. The other end should be tied to the stick about a third of the way from the top.

❷ Then tape the string down to keep it from slipping.

❸ Hold the stick in one hand. Flip the ring into the air and try to catch it on the end of the stick.

❹ Got it? Try tossing it 10 times and score a point for every time you catch the ring. The player with the most points is the winner.

A "Simple" Addition

Try the ring toss using your hand that you don't write with or play this game with your eyes closed.

FORTUNATELY, UNFORTUNATELY

Some people just can't help looking on the sunny side of a situation. Others always seem to have a black cloud over their heads. Here's your chance to look at life from every angle!

WHAT YOU'LL NEED
• two or more players

HOW TO PLAY

❶ The first player begins by making a statement using the word *fortunately*. It can be about anything real or imagined that he or she is happy about. For instance, the game might start with a player saying, "Fortunately, I'm going to the mall today."

❷ The next player then follows up with a sentence using the word *unfortunately*. In the sample here, a response might be, "Unfortunately, I don't have any money." The answer can be silly, as long as it still makes sense, like, "Unfortunately, the mall slid into the ocean last night." Or, "Unfortunately, there's a lion running loose in the parking lot."

❸ Then it's time for the first player to look on the bright side again with a follow-up starting with something like, "Fortunately, I'm a trained lion tamer."

❹ Keep going back and forth until you run out of ideas. Or, if you're having a lot of fun, switch to another story and start over.

SING-ALONG, STRING-ALONG

You probably know a thousand songs—but how fast can you recall one of them when you need to? In this game, you'll have until the count of three to start your melody.

WHAT YOU'LL NEED
• two or more players

HOW TO PLAY

❶ Begin the game by singing any song you choose.

❷ At the end of one of the lines of the song, stop singing. Then point to another player while you count slowly to three.

❸ The player has until you reach "three" to start singing a new song. The trick is: The song has to use one of the words from the last line of the song you just finished. Any word can be used—even a little one like the, an, or of. Suppose you were singing "For He's a Jolly Good Fellow" and ended with the line, "which nobody can deny." The other player must pick up with a song that contains any of those four words.

❹ That player keeps singing, then points to another player, who has till the count of three to take over. Can't think of a new song fast enough? Then you're out of the game. The last player remaining is the winner.

I, NO, YES

Can you buy an imaginary item without ever saying the words I, no, or yes? It's tougher than it seems—especially when your opponent will use every trick in the book to get you to slip.

WHAT YOU'LL NEED
• **two players**
• **timer or watch with second hand**

HOW TO PLAY

❶ One player is the storekeeper and the other is the shopper.

❷ To start the game, the shopper enters the imaginary store and begins to ask the storekeeper questions. The object is to try to get the storekeeper to use the taboo words I, no, or yes in the response. The shopper may ask, "Do you have any pickles?" or "How are you today?" in hopes of getting an answer like "Yes" or "I'm fine"—words that aren't allowed.

❸ The storekeeper must give an answer. The shopper scores a point every time the storekeeper says "I," "No," or "Yes."

❹ After three minutes, the shopper and the storekeeper switch places. The player with the most points is the winner.

SILLY-GRAMS

People send telegrams when they want to get a message out fast. You can play Silly-Grams just when you need a good laugh!

WHAT YOU'LL NEED
• **two or more players** • **several sheets of paper**
• **pens or pencils (one per player)**

HOW TO PLAY

❶ Each player copies the letters from a license plate of a passing car. Leave about two inches between each letter. Trade papers with another player.

❷ Each letter is the first letter in a word in your Silly-Gram! Using the letters and numbers in the order they appear, write a sentence. It has to make sense—even if it's just a silly sort of sense. A few guidelines:

- You can choose to replace numbers with words that rhyme. Three, for example, can be tree, see, flee. Instead of five, you can use hive, chive, or survive.
- It's okay to also use numbers as numbers.
- Tiny words known as "articles" or "conjunctions" can be thrown in wherever you need them. Some samples: a, an, and, the, than, or, to, of, at, for.

❸ Ready to string your sentence together? Suppose your license plate reads STA41G. Your sentence might be, "Silly telegrams are more (rhymes with four) fun (rhymes with one) than (a conjunction) giraffes. When everyone is finished, vote to see who has the goofiest Silly-Gram!

46

HOW LONG TILL WE GET THERE?

Instead of asking the question "How long till we get there?" you'll be giving the answer!

WHAT YOU'LL NEED
• **two or more players** • **paper** • **pen or pencil**

HOW TO PLAY

1 Start by picking an object in the distance that everyone in the car can see. You might choose a billboard, mountain, farmhouse, windmill, tree, or gas station.

2 The driver says "Go," then looks at the odometer, which is the instrument in a car that shows how far it has gone. No one else should peek! In fact, the driver should cover up the odometer if possible.

3 Now each player calls out how far away he or she thinks the object is. One player should record everyone's guesses. The guesses should be made to the nearest tenth of a mile.

4 When you pass the object, the driver reads the exact mileage shown on the odometer. To find out the distance that you traveled, subtract the first odometer reading from this number. The player with the closest guess wins the game.

ALPHABET
SOUP

Don't worry, this isn't a recipe! It's a word-search game that has you hunting for words in a grid just like you hunt for letters in your favorite soup!

WHAT YOU'LL NEED

• two or more players • several sheets of paper
• pens or pencils (one per player) • ruler

GETTING READY

With a ruler, players divide their paper equally into 100 squares (9 lines up and down, 9 lines across).

HOW TO PLAY

❶ Players take turns calling out letters, like *B, Z, A,* or *F.*

❷ As each letter is called, write it in any one of the spaces on your grid.

❸ The object of the game is to form as many words as you can, either up and down, across, or diagonally. When it's your turn to name the letter, choose wisely so that you can add to or complete a word.

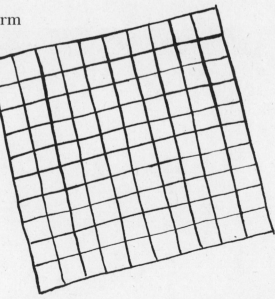

❹ Continue until all players have filled in their 100 squares.

5 Now set a timer for five minutes. Players race to circle as many words as they can find in their grids. It's okay to circle a word within a word. Scat, for example, can count as three words: *scat*, *cat*, and *at*.

6 Now award one point for each word circled. For words using more than four letters, score as follows:

5-letter words	3 points
6-letter words	5 points
7-letter words	8 points
8 or more-letter words	10 points

The player with the most points at the end of the game is the winner.

DREAM
STATE

Even when you're stuck in a traffic jam, this game will keep you moving—even if it's only in your imagination!

WHAT YOU'LL NEED
• two or more players • map or atlas of the United States (optional)
• several sheets of paper • pens or pencils (one per player)

HOW TO PLAY

❶ Get out your map or use the one shown here and pinpoint your starting place. This can be any state, although it's usually easier if you start in the state you're in.

❷ Each player now chooses his or her own Dream State—that's a dream vacation spot at least six states away. Two players can choose the same state, but it's usually more fun and less frustrating to go to different places.

❸ Your goal is to be the first to get to your state by pretending to share the ride with cars bearing license plates of states along the way. Begin the game by looking for a license plate from your home state on the cars around you.

❹ Once you see it, point it out to the other players. Then write it down on your paper. This is your official Trip List. Other players are racing to find the license plates they need at the same time. Be sure to claim your car quickly because no two players can use the same one.

❺ Now you must find a license plate of a bordering state that will continue your trek cross-country. Suppose you decided to travel from Nevada to Indiana. Once you found a license plate for your starting state, you could choose to continue your trip by claiming a plate that you see from California, Utah, Arizona, Idaho, or Oregon, all of which border Nevada.

❻ Write down each state you pass through on your Trip List. You don't have to get to your Dream State using the most direct route. As long as you're moving from one state to another that borders it, you can try to get from Michigan to Florida by way of California, if you think that will get you there the fastest!

❼ The first player to reach his or her Dream State is the winner.

S N A K E S

Try to connect the dots to make a snake, and time won't just fly—it will sssssssslither by!

WHAT YOU'LL NEED

• two or more players • paper • pen or pencil

HOW TO PLAY

1 Make a grid of dots. To do this, draw 5 rows of dots that are each 10 up and down. You'll have a total of 50 dots, just like you see here. This is the board that all players will use. If you want to play a longer game, just make more rows of dots!

2 Start at any dot. Players take turns drawing lines to connect one dot to another. The object of Snakes is to draw lines without ever making a complete square.

3 If you draw a line that makes a box, you lose the game. Try to fill up as much of the grid as possible, and your game will take on the shape of a snake!

LETTER
LADDERS

What do you need to get a really high score in this game? A long, long ladder—of course!

WHAT YOU'LL NEED

• **two or more players** • **several sheets of lined notebook paper**
• **pens or pencils (one per player)** • **dictionary (optional)**
• **timer or watch with a second hand**

HOW TO PLAY

❶ Choose a word that has at least seven letters.

❷ Each player writes the word vertically on the left side of his or her paper with the letters going down. Then the word is repeated on the right side with the letters going up, like you see here.

❸ Each line is called a "ladder." Number each ladder starting at the top from one.

❹ Set your timer for five minutes. Now all players race to create words on each ladder. Your words must begin with the letter on the left-hand side, and end with the letter on the right. Try to think of the longest words possible.

❺ If you're stuck, you can use a dictionary to help think of a word. When the time is up, here's how you add up your score: The player with the longest word for each step on the ladder gets five points for that step. Then players add up the total number of letters used for all their words and give themselves a point for each. The player to reach 100 points first is the winner.

40 GUESS-A-PENNY

The next time a friend offers you "a penny for your thoughts," why not suggest this fast-paced guessing game?

WHAT YOU'LL NEED
• two players • 10 pennies per person

HOW TO PLAY

❶ Start with 10 pennies each. Tuck them in your pockets or somewhere they can't be seen.

❷ One player then holds a secret number of his or her pennies in a closed fist and says, "Guess-a-penny!"

❸ Can you use your extra-centsory perception to guess the number of coins? Give it a try!

❹ If your guess is on the money—that is, exactly right—you get to take all the pennies in your opponent's hand. A guess that's too high or too low, though, means that you must give up the difference from your own stash. Suppose you guessed four pennies but the other player was actually holding seven. Subtract four from seven and hand over three pennies to your opponent.

❺ Take turns guessing. The first player to run out of pennies loses the game.

❻ Store the coins in a game jar so that you'll have plenty of pennies on hand the next time you want to play.

GOING
THE DISTANCE

Place your bets on the car "pool." How far did you go? Only the driver knows!

WHAT YOU'LL NEED

• two or more players • several sheets of paper
• pens or pencils (one per player) • cooperative driver!

HOW TO PLAY

1 Decide how long you want the round to go: Five minutes? The length of a song? Or just let the driver decide.

2 The driver announces when the game begins by saying, "Now!" He or she then checks the odometer, which is the instrument on a car that shows how many miles it has traveled. No one else gets to peek!

3 Get your pen and paper ready. Wait for the driver to say, "Stop!" Each player then quickly writes down how far they think the car has gone. Guesses should be to the nearest tenth of a mile, such as 3.5 miles.

4 When everyone has guessed, the driver announces the actual distance.

5 Your score is the difference between the distance and your guess. If you hit it on the head, you score 0. Otherwise, subtract one amount from the other. For example, if you guessed 1.2 miles and actually traveled 1.5, then your score is .3.

6 Keep playing, adding to your total score. The game ends when you get where you're going or the driver gets tired of playing. The player with the fewest points wins.

55

42

CREATE A
VANITY PLATE

Can you get your point across in seven letters and numbers or less? Make up clever messages just like you see on license plates.

WHAT YOU'LL NEED
• two or more players • several sheets of paper
• pens or pencils (one per player)

HOW TO PLAY

❶ Players take turns coming up with ideas that they'll turn into vanity license plates. Vanity plates are specially ordered plates that—instead of just using random numbers and letters—actually spell out a message. Your vanity plate can be a phrase like "I'm happy," or it can be more general, like a favorite thing to do or foods that are yummy.

❷ Now try to invent a license plate that describes your idea in seven letters and numbers or less. It can be just a word, like HAPPYME. Or you can combine letters with numbers, such as IFLGR8, which—when sounded out—says "I feel great!"

❸ It's not always easy to get a big idea into seven letters or numbers. Some tips are:

- You don't always have to use vowels. *CHK* looks enough like *check* or *chick*, or *ZP* like *zip*.
- Think of how words sound. *View* can be *VU* or *follow* can be *FALO*.
- Use numbers to substitute for words that sound similar.

> 1—*won* as well as *one*
>
> 2—*to* and *too*
>
> 4—*for*
>
> 8—*ate*

- Get really creative and combine letters with numbers to make words. An *S* in front of *2* (S2) makes *stew*. *PL* in front of *8* is *plate* (PL8). A *K* after *4* (4K) is *fork*!

❹ Set a time limit, then vote on whose license plate says it best!

43 PLATE
COLLECTORS

This is one of those games that you can play even on the longest road trip and never finish . . . or get bored! Stay on the lookout for license plates from different states. You can even be a plate collector while you're playing other travel games.

WHAT YOU'LL NEED

• one or more players • map or atlas of the United States
• several sheets of lined notebook paper • pens or pencils (one per player)

HOW TO PLAY

❶ Draw a line down the center of your paper to make two columns. Label one column "states" and the other "mottos." You'll probably need to use both sides of your paper.

❷ Now consult your map as you write down all 50 states and the District of Columbia under the heading "states." Put stars next to Hawaii and Alaska. To play, look at the license plates on passing cars. The aim of the game is to try to get one from each state on your list.

❸ When you spot one, be the first to point it out. Then circle the name of the state on your list. Does the license plate also have a motto? These appear on some plates, like "Michigan, the Great Lakes State." If so, list it in the right-hand column, next to the state.

❹ If one player finds all 50 states, it's time for all players to tally their points. It's very likely no one will find all the states, so you can set a time for the game to end.

❺ Award one point for each state that you found. Add two more points for each motto. If you spotted plates from Hawaii or Alaska (easy if you live there!), give yourself five points for each of these instead of just one. The player with the most points at the end of the game wins.

CRAZY ACTS
OF KINDNESS

Doing something nice for your fellow travelers can really do wonders for lifting their spirits as well as your own.

HOW TO PLAY

❶ The fun part about Crazy Acts of Kindness is that people don't expect them. Start by just keeping an eye out for a chance to do a good deed. This isn't about saving people from burning buildings (that only happens once in a lifetime, if ever)! It's about the little things you can do every day to bring a smile to a friend or a stranger's face.

❷ Stuck for ideas? Here are a few to get you started. As you travel through your day, you'll probably think of more:

- Offer your seat on the bus or the train to a traveler who looks like he or she could use a rest.
- Let a fellow shopper go ahead of you in line.
- Let your sister or brother read your new magazine before you do.
- Hold a restaurant door open for someone.
- Send a postcard to a former teacher with a note saying how he or she made a difference in your life.

❸ There's no end to this game. No matter how long you play, everybody comes out a winner!

NOTE: *Never approach a stranger by yourself. A parent or other adult should be with you at all times!*

GIVE ME
A HAND

Got time on your hands? Here's a game that's great to play while you're taking a stretch from a car, on a layover at the airport, or in your hotel room.

WHAT YOU'LL NEED
• two or more players

HOW TO PLAY

❶ Stand face-to-face with another player at arm's length. Each player's feet should be together.

❷ To get in the ready position, push your arms forward with your wrists bent up like you see here. You should be palm-to-palm with your opponent.

❸ Count together to three. Then using only your hands, try to knock the other player off balance while he or she does the same to you. It's okay to wobble around or let go of hands. Never, however, make contact with any part of the other player's body except for the hands.

❹ Start the game with five points each and as you play, score as follows:

- A player who moves one or both feet loses a point.
- Tipping over and grabbing onto the other player also costs you a point.
- For falling completely, subtract two points.
- No points are lost if both players fall or move their feet at the same time.

The first player to score 0 loses the game.

CAR
COLLECTING

46

Car collecting is a hobby usually reserved for the rich and famous. This game gives you a taste of the glamorous life—without spending a dime!

WHAT YOU'LL NEED
• two or more players • timer or watch

HOW TO PLAY

❶ Each player chooses a make of car or truck, such as Honda, Nissan, Ford, or Chrysler. Now pick a lucky color that will be yours throughout the game. Set a time limit, such as 15 minutes.

❷ Watch as cars and trucks pass by. Try to spot as many of the make you chose as you can. Parked cars count, as do cars being towed and pictures of cars on billboards.

❸ If you spy a car that's the right make, show it to the other players. Then give yourself a point. If the car or truck is in your lucky color, you get a bonus point.

❹ When time's up, the player with the most points wins.

ANIMAL FARM CARDS

If you're playing this game in a hotel—be careful! You don't want the other guests complaining that it sounds like they're on a farm!

WHAT YOU'LL NEED

• **three or more players**
• **deck of playing cards**

HOW TO PLAY

❶ Before you start, each player chooses a different animal to imitate. You might want to moo like a cow, quack like a duck, or screech like a monkey.

❷ Don't forget what animal you are. You also need to remember the sounds chosen by the other players. Pick one player to be the dealer and someone who'll go first.

❸ The dealer shuffles the cards and deals the entire deck facedown around the table. Each player should have a little pile in front of him or her.

❹ First, take a card from the pile in front of you. Lay it down faceup right beside your other stack of cards, so everyone can see. This will be your discard pile.

5 In clockwise order, each player does the same. Watch closely! If you lay down a card that's the same as the one on top of someone else's discard pile, quickly make the animal noise of the other player. For example, if the "pig" lays down a 7 that matches the 7 on the pile of the "bird," the pig tries to chirp before the bird can oink.

6 The player who correctly makes the other player's animal noise first gets all the cards in the other player's discard pile.

7 The game starts up again when the player who lost his or her discard pile lays down a new card.

8 If you lose all your cards, you're out of the game. The last player left will have all 52 cards and is the winner.

48 ROUND-THE-CLOCK

Throw dice in the order of numbers on the clock, and watch time fly by!

WHAT YOU'LL NEED

• **two or more players** • **two dice** • **paper** • **pen or pencil**
• **tiny game piece for each player, such as a bead, a rock, or a coin**
• **tray or box lid (optional)**

HOW TO PLAY

1 Draw a large circle on a sheet of paper. Write numbers on it from 1 to 12 so that it looks like a clock. Set your clock on a sturdy surface so that it's easy to move your game pieces around. Start with all your game pieces on 12 o'clock on your board.

2 The first player rolls both dice to try to get a 1 on either of the die. If a 1 appears, you can move your game piece to 1 o'clock. If not, it's the next player's turn. Each player gets one roll per turn.

3 After you roll a 1, you can try for 2, then 3, and so on. You have to get the numbers in order—rolling a 4 doesn't count unless you've already gotten 1, 2, and 3. Some rules are:

- You can use a number that appears on either of the dice thrown.
- You can also add up the numbers of both dice—so if you need 5 and you roll a 2 and a 3, you can move your game piece forward on the clock.

4 For 7 through 12 o'clock, add up both dice thrown. However, it's the total number of dots showing that count—a 1 and 1 don't make 11, they only add up to 2. The first player to make it round-the-clock from 1 to 12 wins the game.

THE MIME
RHYME

Your parents might like the idea of a nice quiet game where you imitate a mime! The only problem: Your friends might get pretty giggly as they call out answers to lead you to a clue.

WHAT YOU'LL NEED
• **two or more players**

HOW TO PLAY

1 Choose one player to be the mime. To start, the mime covers his or her ears. The rest of the players whisper to decide on a word that the mime must guess. Pick a simple word that can easily be rhymed.

HE'S GOOD!

2 Players now tell the mime to guess the word. They offer a hint by giving a word that the secret word rhymes with. For instance, if the word is pie, players might say, "It rhymes with try."

3 Of course, mimes don't talk, so the only way to answer is to act it out. The mime might pretend to wipe big tears away, for example, to stand for cry. The others tell him or her that's not the correct word. The mime then might pretend to be stabbed and fall over, as in die. This goes on until the mime gets the word right. Then it's time for another player to be the mime.

4 Keep track of how many guesses the mime made. After everyone has taken a turn as the mime, the player who guessed in the fewest number of mimes wins the game.

OPPOSITES
ATTRACT

Do as you're told—that is, unless you're playing Opposites Attract!

WHAT YOU'LL NEED

• **three or more players**

HOW TO PLAY

1 Choose one person to be the caller. The game starts when the caller gives a command. He or she might say, "Stick out your tongue." The caller should speak clearly but not act out any of the motions. If you are playing in the car, all players need to keep in mind what can and can't be done in a moving vehicle, as well as to consider the comfort of the driver.

2 Now instead of doing what you're told, do just the opposite! Don't raise your right arm—lower it. Don't jump up—squat down. If the caller says, "Clap your hands," clap your feet or wave your hands past each other without touching. (Sometimes the opposite will depend on what you think best shows that you're *not* obeying orders.)

3 Always be careful because the caller will be watching! If he or she sees you accidentally following instructions, you're out of the game. The last player left wins and gets to be the caller for the next round.

MAGAZINE
MEMORY

Pit the power of your brain against your friend's brain. Who has the best memory?

WHAT YOU'LL NEED
• two players • magazine • several sheets of paper
• pens or pencils (one per player) • timer or watch

HOW TO PLAY

❶ Ask someone who's not playing to look through a magazine to find a page that has a picture with a lot of details.

❷ Open the magazine to that page so that both players can see it well. Set your timer for one minute and each player stares at it, memorizing as many details as possible. When the minute is up, close the magazine.

❸ You now have three minutes to write down everything you can remember from the picture. When the time is up, check your answers against the picture.

❹ Score one point for each item there, and subtract a point if you wrote down something that wasn't really in the picture. The person with the most points wins.

TABLETOP
FOOTBALL

Nothing beats the excitement of football! All you need for this version of the game is a table and a plain piece of paper.

WHAT YOU'LL NEED
• two players • piece of 8½" x 11" paper
• table (ideally about 3 feet long) • paper • pen or pencil

GETTING STARTED

❶ You can't play football without the ole pigskin! To make one, fold a piece of paper in half lengthwise. Then fold it over lengthwise again.

❷ Bring the top-left corner down so that it forms a triangle like you see here. Repeat this step with the top-right corner, then the left, and so on, just like you would fold a flag.

❸ Tuck the bottom edge into the open flap to secure the "football."

HOW TO PLAY

❶ Each player claims half of the table. Start by
setting the football on your edge of the table.

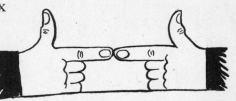

❷ To put the ball in play, flick it with your finger
or give it a shove. The goal is to get it to the other
side of the table so that it's hanging slightly over
the edge, without falling off. That's considered a
"touchdown." If it falls to the ground, that's a "down."
Anywhere else on the table just keeps the ball in play.

❸ Opposing players usually "throw" the ball from the point where it
landed. The exception is a down, after which you can set the ball
anywhere on your side of the table.

❹ While playing, you may have the chance to try for a "field goal." In
tabletop football, this happens after a touchdown, or after the other
player gets three downs. In field-goal kicking, the other player serves as
the goal posts by putting his or her index
fingers together and thumbs up like
you see here. Now set the ball 3 inches
from the edge of the table. Try to flick
it above the goal post (the fingers) and
between the thumbs.

❺ Keep score as you go along. Scoring is as follows:

field goal after a touchdown	1 point
field goal after 3 downs	3 points
touchdown	6 points

❻ The winner is the first player to reach 30 points, or, if you can't play that
long, the one with the highest score.

ACTION
BEE

So you think spelling bees are a breeze? Here's a game that'll have you on your toes and will really get your blood pumping after a long ride.

WHAT YOU'LL NEED
• **four or more players** • **dictionary** • **paper** • **pen or pencil**

HOW TO PLAY

❶ With the other players, make a list of seven letters that will be replaced by actions. *C* may be a clap, *K* may be a kick, *H* a hop, *J* a jumping jack, and so on.

❷ Choose one player to be the teacher. To begin, the teacher gives the first player a word to spell. You must not only spell the word correctly but also replace letters with the chosen actions. If the word is "pickle," for example, you might say "P-I" then clap for *C*, kick for *K*, and say "L-E."

❸ If you get it right, you remain in the game and the next player gets a chance to spell a word. If you miss a motion or spell the word wrong, you're O-U-T, out.

❹ The last player who correctly action-spells a word wins the round and gets a turn to be the teacher.

L E A P F R O G

Just like tic-tac-toe, this game has you trying to get three in a row—but it keeps going where tic-tac-toe leaves off!

WHAT YOU'LL NEED

**• paper • pen or pencil • ruler • four tiny game pieces,
such as beads, rocks, or coins (two of one kind and two of another)**

HOW TO PLAY

❶ Draw a big square in the center of your paper.

❷ Now draw diagonal lines to form an X, and one across the exact middle. Your game board should look like what you see here.

❸ To begin, each of you takes turns placing one piece at a time on the board. You can put a piece on any point where two or more lines meet.

❹ Has the last piece been set down? Now you move pieces in turn, trying to get three in a row in any direction: up and down, across, or diagonally. You can move from one point to the next, or jump another piece, just like in checkers. The first player to get three in a row is the winner.

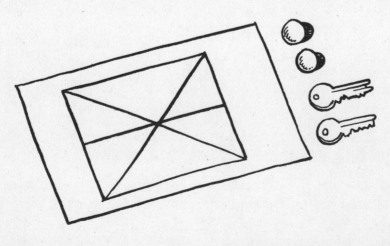

55

THUMB
WRESTLING

Here's a classic contest you'll give a big thumbs-up. Even the biggest, scariest foe won't stand a chance against your thumbs of steel!

WHAT YOU'LL NEED
• **two players**

HOW TO PLAY

1 Hold your right hand out as if to shake hands. The other player does the same so that his or her fingertips are just touching yours.

2 Now link hands by curving your fingers and hooking them into your opponent's hand, like you see here. Your thumb should be flat against your hand.

3 To begin the match, count aloud to three while doing the following:

• One . . . Lift your thumb so that it points up, then lay it back down.
• Two . . . Move your thumb to the right so that it crosses over the other player's thumb.
• Three . . . Touch the thumb back to where it started, flat against your hand, then lift it to begin the battle.

4 Now, as fast as you can, try to pin the other player's thumb to his or her hand by pushing against it with your own thumb.

5 Once a player pins the other's thumb, he or she wins the match. The player who wins the most out of five matches is the thumb wrestling champion.

COFFEEPOT

There's nothing like a fun-filled game of Coffeepot to "perk" up a boring car ride!

WHAT YOU'LL NEED

• three or more players

HOW TO PLAY

❶ First choose a verb and keep it in your head. It can be any action word, such as *cry, run, carry, sneeze, trip, drive, park* and so on. Don't let anyone else know what it is!

❷ Now players take turns asking yes or no questions to try to guess the verb. Since they don't know what it is yet, however, they have to substitute the word *coffeepot* in their questions. This makes even the most simple question sound really silly. For example, they might ask, "Can you coffeepot outside?" "Do birds coffeepot?" "Do kids coffeepot at school?" "Have you ever coffeepotted?"

❸ Answer each question with a yes or no. If the verb is *talk*, then you might answer yes to someone who asks if you can coffeepot in the dark but no to someone who asks if alligators can coffeepot.

❹ Once a player is pretty sure what *coffeepot* really means, he or she can call out a guess. Each player gets three guesses. After that, they're out of the game.

❺ The first player to identify the verb is the winner and gets to choose the secret meaning of *coffeepot* for the next round.

While everyone else is asleep, here's an activity that can keep you going around in circles for hours!

WHAT YOU'LL NEED
• construction paper • large sheet of plain white paper
• compass (the type used to make circles) • pen or pencil • scissors • paper

BEFORE YOU LEAVE

❶ First use your compass to make seven disks on construction paper. You'll need one disk each that is 4, 5, 6, 7, 8, 9, and 10 inches around. Cut out the disks and set them aside.

❷ Now, on your white paper, draw three 10-inch circles side by side like you see here. Label them 1, 2, and 3.

NOTE: *Never use scissors in a moving vehicle, especially a car, bus, or train. Cut out what you need before you leave.*

HOW TO PLAY

❶ Stack the disks on the circle marked 1. The largest should be on the bottom and the smallest on top.

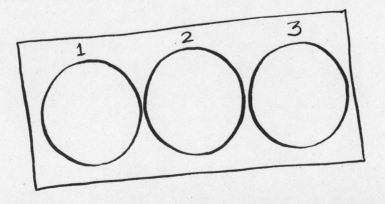

❷ The idea of the game is simple: to transfer the stack of disks from the first circle to the third using as few moves as possible. Some rules are:

- You can't place a disk on top of one that's smaller.
- You can only move one disk at a time.
- It's okay to move forward or backward.
- You can only move to the next circle. For example, you can shift a disk from circle 1 to 2, but not from 1 to 3.

❸ Keep count as you move disks. Each move counts as a point, whether you're moving forward or backward. When all the disks are on circle 3, in order from the biggest on the bottom to the smallest on the top, whatever number of move you were on when you got there is your total score.

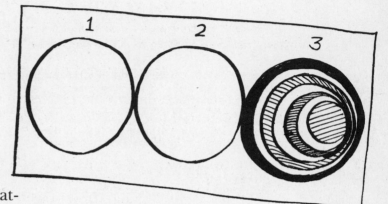

❹ Play against your best score, or take turns with other players to try to beat their best scores.

BACKWARD
WORDS

Can you recognize a word if it's said backward? Some say this game is really fun—others think that it's "nuf yllaer!"

WHAT YOU'LL NEED
• two or more players • several sheets of paper
• pens or pencils (one per player)

HOW TO PLAY

❶ Start by writing down the name of a simple object. Some examples are: purse, tomato, pencil, glasses, eggs, horse. Don't let the other players see what you wrote.

❷ Say your word aloud . . . *backward*. If the word is *dollar*, for example, say "rallod." To be fair, don't change how vowels sound, and speak slowly and clearly.

❸ The other players now try to figure out the word and call out their guesses. You can tell the players your word up to five times, but they aren't allowed to write anything down.

RAC SPIRT ELUR!

❹ The first player to guess the word gets a point. If no one can guess the word after you've said it five times, you get a point.

❺ Players take turns making up backward words. After three rounds, the player with the most points wins.

Take a long look at an ordinary item and you'll find there's more there than meets the eye.

WHAT YOU'LL NEED
• **two or more players** • **several sheets of paper**
• **pens or pencils (one per player)** • **common household item**

HOW TO PLAY

❶ Select an ordinary household item that you'll use for this game. It might be a paper clip, a pencil, a spoon, soap, keys, a paper cup, or a potato. Place the item so that it can clearly be seen by all players.

❷ Now everyone makes his or her own list of all the ways the item could possibly be used. Think you can only use keys to open a door? How about to scratch a design in a stone, make a necklace, or poke a hole in a piece of plastic wrap? Don't be afraid to write down all your ideas, even if they seem silly.

❸ Read your ideas aloud. Count up who has the most. Also vote for who invented an idea that was the craziest, one that was the most creative, and one that was the most sensible.

TRAVEL
TIMELINE

Think souvenirs have to cost a lot of money? This game has you collecting some pretty strange stuff on your travels.

WHAT YOU'LL NEED
• **paper and pencil** • **storage bag**

HOW TO PLAY

❶ Each time you and your friends or family make a stop on your vacation, try to find a souvenir. The trick is: It must be free and, of course, okay for you to take. Don't let anyone else see what you're collecting. Some ideas to get you started:

- Look for free postcards or stationery at hotels.
- Hang on to the maps from theme parks.
- Keep the programs or ticket stubs from shows you see.
- Grab matches, napkins, or even paper cups from restaurants.
- Keep bus transfer tickets, plane boarding passes, or train ticket stubs.
- Pour some beach sand into a small container.
- Pick up a leaf from a particularly pretty tree near your hotel room.

❷ Store your souvenirs in a bag. Write down where you got each item and the order in which you got it—just in case you forget!

❸ After your vacation is over, spread out the contents of your bag. Compare with friends or family members. Who found the most stuff?

❹ Now, without peeking at your list, try to arrange all your items in the order you found them. This is your Travel Timeline and is a creative way to remember what a great time you had on your getaway.

❺ You can arrange items permanently on a big board. Or you can even combine your findings with other family members to make one big Family Travel Timeline.

HAPPY TRAILS!